2021-22 JULY - DECEMBER PLANNER

NAME

PHONE

EMAIL

ADDRESS

EMERGENCY CONTACTS

NAME
PHONE
EMAIL
ADDRESS

NAME
PHONE
EMAIL
ADDRESS

NAME
PHONE
EMAIL
ADDRESS

NAME
PHONE
EMAIL
ADDRESS

EMERGENCY CONTACTS

NAME
PHONE
EMAIL
ADDRESS

NAME
PHONE
EMAIL
ADDRESS

NAME
PHONE
EMAIL
ADDRESS

NAME
PHONE
EMAIL
ADDRESS

2021

JANUARY
M	T	W	T	F	S	S
				1	**2**	3
4	5	6	7	8	**9**	10
11	12	13	14	15	**16**	17
18	19	20	21	22	**23**	24
25	26	27	28	29	**30**	31

FEBRUARY
M	T	W	T	F	S	S
1	2	3	**4**	5	6	7
8	9	10	11	12	13	14
15	16	17	18	19	20	21
22	23	24	25	26	27	28

MARCH
M	T	W	T	F	S	S
1	2	3	4	5	6	7
8	9	10	11	12	13	14
15	16	17	18	19	20	21
22	23	24	25	26	27	28
29	30	31				

APRIL
M	T	W	T	F	S	S
			1	2	3	4
5	6	7	8	9	10	11
12	13	14	15	16	17	18
19	20	21	22	23	24	25
26	27	28	29	30		

MAY
M	T	W	T	F	S	S
					1	**2**
3	4	5	**6**	**7**	8	**9**
10	11	12	**13**	**14**	15	**16**
17	18	19	**20**	**21**	22	**23**
24	25	26	**27**	**28**	29	**30**
31						

JUNE
M	T	W	T	F	S	S
	1	2	3	4	5	6
7	8	9	10	**11**	12	13
14	15	16	17	**18**	19	20
21	22	23	24	**25**	26	27
28	29	30				

JULY
M	T	W	T	F	S	S
			1	2	3	4
5	6	7	8	9	10	11
12	13	14	15	16	17	18
19	20	21	22	23	24	25
26	27	28	29	30		

AUGUST
M	T	W	T	F	S	S
					7	1
2	3	4	5	6	**7**	8
9	10	11	12	13	**14**	15
16	17	18	19	20	**21**	22
23	24	25	26	27	**28**	29
30	31					

SEPTEMBER
M	T	W	T	F	S	S
		1	2	3	4	5
6	7	8	9	10	11	12
13	14	15	16	17	18	19
20	21	22	23	24	25	26
27	28	29	30			

OCTOBER
M	T	W	T	F	S	S
				1	2	3
4	5	6	**7**	8	9	10
11	12	13	**14**	15	16	17
18	19	20	**21**	22	23	24
25	26	27	**28**	29	30	31

NOVEMBER
M	T	W	T	F	S	S
1	2	3	4	5	**6**	7
8	9	10	11	12	**13**	14
15	16	17	18	19	**20**	21
22	23	24	25	26	**27**	28
29	30					

DECEMBER
M	T	W	T	F	S	S
		1	2	3	4	5
6	7	8	9	10	11	12
13	14	15	16	17	18	19
20	21	22	23	24	25	26
27	28	29	30	31		

2022

JANUARY
M	T	W	T	F	S	S
					1	2
3	4	5	**6**	**7**	8	9
10	11	12	**13**	**14**	15	16
17	18	19	**20**	**21**	22	23
24	25	26	**27**	**28**	29	30
31						

FEBRUARY
M	T	W	T	F	S	S
	1	2	3	4	5	6
7	8	9	10	11	12	13
14	15	16	17	18	19	20
21	22	23	24	25	26	27
28						

MARCH
M	T	W	T	F	S	S
	1	2	3	4	5	6
7	8	9	10	11	12	13
14	15	16	17	18	19	20
21	22	23	24	25	26	27
28	29	30	31			

APRIL
M	T	W	T	F	S	S
				1	2	3
4	5	6	**7**	8	9	10
11	12	13	**14**	15	16	17
18	19	20	**21**	22	23	24
25	26	27	**28**	29	30	

MAY
M	T	W	T	F	S	S
						1
2	3	4	**5**	6	**7**	8
9	10	11	**12**	13	**14**	15
16	17	18	**19**	20	**21**	22
23	24	25	**26**	27	**28**	29
30	31					

JUNE
M	T	W	T	F	S	S
		1	2	3	4	5
6	7	8	9	10	11	12
13	14	15	16	17	18	19
20	21	22	23	24	25	26
27	28	29	30			

JULY
M	T	W	T	F	S	S
				1	2	3
4	5	6	7	8	9	10
11	12	13	14	15	16	17
18	19	20	21	22	23	24
25	26	27	28	29	30	31

AUGUST
M	T	W	T	F	S	S
1	2	3	4	**5**	6	7
8	9	10	11	**12**	13	14
15	16	17	18	**19**	20	21
22	23	24	25	**26**	27	28
29	30	31				

SEPTEMBER
M	T	W	T	F	S	S
			1	2	3	4
5	6	7	8	9	10	11
12	13	14	15	16	17	18
19	20	21	22	23	24	25
26	27	28	29	30		

OCTOBER
M	T	W	T	F	S	S
					1	2
3	4	5	6	**7**	8	9
10	11	12	13	**14**	15	16
17	18	19	20	**21**	22	23
24	25	26	27	**28**	29	30
31						

NOVEMBER
M	T	W	T	F	S	S
	1	2	3	4	5	6
7	8	9	10	11	12	13
14	15	16	17	18	19	20
21	22	23	24	25	26	27
28	29	30				

DECEMBER
M	T	W	T	F	S	S
			1	2	3	4
5	6	7	8	9	10	11
12	13	14	15	16	17	18
19	20	21	22	23	24	25
26	27	28	29	30	31	

2023

JANUARY
M	T	W	T	F	S	S
						1
2	3	4	5	6	**7**	8
9	10	11	12	13	**14**	15
16	17	18	19	20	**21**	22
23	24	25	26	27	**28**	29
30	31					

FEBRUARY
M	T	W	T	F	S	S
		1	2	3	4	5
6	7	8	9	10	11	12
13	14	15	16	17	18	19
20	21	22	23	24	25	26
27	28					

MARCH
M	T	W	T	F	S	S
		1	2	3	4	5
6	7	8	9	10	11	12
13	14	15	16	17	18	19
20	21	22	23	24	25	26
27	28	29	30	31		

APRIL
M	T	W	T	F	S	S
					1	2
3	4	5	6	7	8	9
10	11	12	13	**14**	15	16
17	18	19	20	**21**	22	23
24	25	26	27	**28**	29	30

MAY
M	T	W	T	F	S	S
1	2	3	4	5	6	7
8	9	10	11	12	13	14
15	16	17	18	19	20	21
22	23	24	25	26	27	28
29	30	31				

JUNE
M	T	W	T	F	S	S
			1	2	3	4
5	6	7	8	9	10	11
12	13	14	15	16	17	18
19	20	21	22	23	24	25
26	27	28	29	30		

JULY
M	T	W	T	F	S	S
					1	2
3	4	5	6	7	8	9
10	11	12	13	14	15	16
17	18	19	20	21	22	23
24	25	26	27	28	29	30
31						

AUGUST
M	T	W	T	F	S	S
	1	2	3	4	5	6
7	8	9	10	11	12	13
14	15	16	17	18	19	20
21	22	23	24	25	26	27
28	29	30	31			

SEPTEMBER
M	T	W	T	F	S	S
				1	2	3
4	5	6	7	8	9	10
11	12	13	14	15	16	17
18	19	20	21	22	23	24
25	26	27	28	29	30	

OCTOBER
M	T	W	T	F	S	S
						1
2	3	4	5	6	**7**	8
9	10	11	12	13	**14**	15
16	17	18	19	20	**21**	22
23	24	25	26	27	**28**	29
30	31					

NOVEMBER
M	T	W	T	F	S	S
		1	2	3	4	5
6	7	8	9	10	11	12
13	14	15	16	17	18	19
20	21	22	23	24	25	26
27	28	29	30			

DECEMBER
M	T	W	T	F	S	S
				1	2	3
4	5	6	**7**	8	9	10
11	12	13	**14**	15	16	17
18	19	20	**21**	22	23	24
25	26	27	**28**	29	30	31

JULY

DATE	DON'T FORGET

AUGUST

DATE	DON'T FORGET

SEPTEMBER

DATE	DON'T FORGET

OCTOBER

DATE	DON'T FORGET

NOVEMBER

DATE	DON'T FORGET

DECEMBER

DATE	DON'T FORGET

JANUARY

DATE	DON'T FORGET

FEBRUARY

DATE	DON'T FORGET

DATE	DON'T FORGET	MARCH

APRIL

DATE	DON'T FORGET

MAY

DATE	DON'T FORGET

JUNE

DATE	DON'T FORGET

DATE	DON'T FORGET

JULY

AUGUST

DATE	DON'T FORGET

SEPTEMBER

DATE	DON'T FORGET

OCTOBER

DATE	DON'T FORGET

NOVEMBER

DATE	DON'T FORGET

DECEMBER

DATE	DON'T FORGET

JANUARY

DATE	DON'T FORGET

JUNE/JULY

28 MONDAY

29 TUESDAY

30 WEDNESDAY

1 THURSDAY

JULY

FRIDAY 2

SATURDAY 3

SUNDAY 4

NOTES

JULY

5 MONDAY

6 TUESDAY

7 WEDNESDAY

8 THURSDAY

JULY

FRIDAY 9

SATURDAY 10

SUNDAY 11

NOTES

JULY

12 MONDAY

13 TUESDAY

14 WEDNESDAY

15 THURSDAY

JULY

FRIDAY 16

SATURDAY 17

SUNDAY 18

NOTES

JULY

19 MONDAY

20 TUESDAY

21 WEDNESDAY

22 THURSDAY

JULY

FRIDAY 23

SATURDAY 24

SUNDAY 25

NOTES

JULY

26 MONDAY

27 TUESDAY

28 WEDNESDAY

29 THURSDAY

JULY/AUGUST

FRIDAY 30

SATURDAY 31

SUNDAY 1

NOTES

AUGUST

2 MONDAY

3 TUESDAY

4 WEDNESDAY

5 THURSDAY

AUGUST

FRIDAY 6

SATURDAY 7

SUNDAY 8

NOTES

AUGUST

9 MONDAY

10 TUESDAY

11 WEDNESDAY

12 THURSDAY

AUGUST

FRIDAY 13

SATURDAY 14

SUNDAY 15

NOTES

AUGUST

16 MONDAY

17 TUESDAY

18 WEDNESDAY

19 THURSDAY

AUGUST

FRIDAY 20

SATURDAY 21

SUNDAY 22

NOTES

AUGUST

23 MONDAY

24 TUESDAY

25 WEDNESDAY

26 THURSDAY

AUGUST

FRIDAY 27

SATURDAY 28

SUNDAY 29

NOTES

AUGUST/SEPTEMBER

30 MONDAY

31 TUESDAY

1 WEDNESDAY

2 THURSDAY

SEPTEMBER

FRIDAY 3

SATURDAY 4

SUNDAY 5

NOTES

SEPTEMBER

6 MONDAY

7 TUESDAY

8 WEDNESDAY

9 THURSDAY

SEPTEMBER

FRIDAY 10

SATURDAY 11

SUNDAY 12

NOTES

SEPTEMBER

13 MONDAY

14 TUESDAY

15 WEDNESDAY

16 THURSDAY

SEPTEMBER

FRIDAY 17

SATURDAY 18

SUNDAY 19

NOTES

SEPTEMBER

20 MONDAY

21 TUESDAY

22 WEDNESDAY

23 THURSDAY

SEPTEMBER

FRIDAY 24

SATURDAY 25

SUNDAY 26

NOTES

SEPTEMBER

27 MONDAY

28 TUESDAY

29 WEDNESDAY

30 THURSDAY

OCTOBER

FRIDAY 1

SATURDAY 2

SUNDAY 3

NOTES

OCTOBER

4 MONDAY

5 TUESDAY

6 WEDNESDAY

7 THURSDAY

OCTOBER

FRIDAY 8

SATURDAY 9

SUNDAY 10

NOTES

OCTOBER

11 MONDAY

12 TUESDAY

13 WEDNESDAY

14 THURSDAY

OCTOBER

FRIDAY 15

SATURDAY 16

SUNDAY 17

NOTES

OCTOBER

18 MONDAY

19 TUESDAY

20 WEDNESDAY

21 THURSDAY

OCTOBER

FRIDAY 22

SATURDAY 23

SUNDAY 24

NOTES

OCTOBER

25 MONDAY

26 TUESDAY

27 WEDNESDAY

28 THURSDAY

OCTOBER

FRIDAY 29

SATURDAY 30

SUNDAY 31

NOTES

NOVEMBER

1 MONDAY

2 TUESDAY

3 WEDNESDAY

4 THURSDAY

NOVEMBER

FRIDAY 5

SATURDAY 6

SUNDAY 7

NOTES

NOVEMBER

8 MONDAY

9 TUESDAY

10 WEDNESDAY

11 THURSDAY

NOVEMBER

FRIDAY 12

SATURDAY 13

SUNDAY 14

NOTES

NOVEMBER

15 MONDAY

16 TUESDAY

17 WEDNESDAY

18 THURSDAY

NOVEMBER

FRIDAY 19

SATURDAY 20

SUNDAY 21

NOTES

NOVEMBER

22 MONDAY

23 TUESDAY

24 WEDNESDAY

25 THURSDAY

NOVEMBER

FRIDAY 26

SATURDAY 27

SUNDAY 28

NOTES

NOVEMBER/DECEMBER

29 MONDAY

30 TUESDAY

1 WEDNESDAY

2 THURSDAY

DECEMBER

FRIDAY 3

SATURDAY 4

SUNDAY 5

NOTES

DECEMBER

6 MONDAY

7 TUESDAY

8 WEDNESDAY

9 THURSDAY

DECEMBER

FRIDAY 10

SATURDAY 11

SUNDAY 12

NOTES

DECEMBER

13 MONDAY

14 TUESDAY

15 WEDNESDAY

16 THURSDAY

DECEMBER

FRIDAY 17

SATURDAY 18

SUNDAY 19

NOTES

DECEMBER

20 MONDAY

21 TUESDAY

22 WEDNESDAY

23 THURSDAY

DECEMBER

FRIDAY 24

SATURDAY 25

SUNDAY 26

NOTES

DECEMBER

27 MONDAY

28 TUESDAY

29 WEDNESDAY

30 THURSDAY

DECEMBER/JANUARY

FRIDAY 31

SATURDAY 1

SUNDAY 2

NOTES

JANUARY

3 MONDAY

4 TUESDAY

5 WEDNESDAY

6 THURSDAY

JANUARY

FRIDAY 7

SATURDAY 8

SUNDAY 9

NOTES

JANUARY

10 MONDAY

11 TUESDAY

12 WEDNESDAY

13 THURSDAY

JANUARY

FRIDAY 14

SATURDAY 15

SUNDAY 16

NOTES

JANUARY

17 MONDAY

18 TUESDAY

19 WEDNESDAY

20 THURSDAY

JANUARY

FRIDAY 21

SATURDAY 22

SUNDAY 23

NOTES

JANUARY

24 MONDAY

25 TUESDAY

26 WEDNESDAY

27 THURSDAY

JANUARY

FRIDAY 28

SATURDAY 29

SUNDAY 30

NOTES

JANUARY/FEBRUARY

31 MONDAY

1 TUESDAY

2 WEDNESDAY

3 THURSDAY

FEBRUARY

FRIDAY 4

SATURDAY 5

SUNDAY 6

NOTES

FEBRUARY

7 MONDAY

8 TUESDAY

9 WEDNESDAY

10 THURSDAY

FEBRUARY

FRIDAY 11

SATURDAY 12

SUNDAY 13

NOTES

FEBRUARY

14 MONDAY

15 TUESDAY

16 WEDNESDAY

17 THURSDAY

FEBRUARY

FRIDAY 18

SATURDAY 19

SUNDAY 20

NOTES

FEBRUARY

21 MONDAY

22 TUESDAY

23 WEDNESDAY

24 THURSDAY

FEBRUARY

FRIDAY 25

SATURDAY 26

SUNDAY 27

NOTES

FEBRUARY/MARCH

28 MONDAY

1 TUESDAY

2 WEDNESDAY

3 THURSDAY

MARCH

FRIDAY 4

SATURDAY 5

SUNDAY 6

NOTES

MARCH

7 MONDAY

8 TUESDAY

9 WEDNESDAY

10 THURSDAY

MARCH

FRIDAY 11

SATURDAY 12

SUNDAY 13

NOTES

MARCH

14 MONDAY

15 TUESDAY

16 WEDNESDAY

17 THURSDAY

MARCH

FRIDAY 18

SATURDAY 19

SUNDAY 20

NOTES

MARCH

21 MONDAY

22 TUESDAY

23 WEDNESDAY

24 THURSDAY

MARCH

FRIDAY 25

SATURDAY 26

SUNDAY 27

NOTES

MARCH

28 MONDAY

29 TUESDAY

30 WEDNESDAY

31 THURSDAY

APRIL

FRIDAY 1

SATURDAY 2

SUNDAY 3

NOTES

APRIL

4 MONDAY

5 TUESDAY

6 WEDNESDAY

7 THURSDAY

APRIL

FRIDAY 8

SATURDAY 9

SUNDAY 10

NOTES

APRIL

11 MONDAY

12 TUESDAY

13 WEDNESDAY

14 THURSDAY

APRIL

FRIDAY 15

SATURDAY 16

SUNDAY 17

NOTES

APRIL

18 MONDAY

19 TUESDAY

20 WEDNESDAY

21 THURSDAY

APRIL

FRIDAY 22

SATURDAY 23

SUNDAY 24

NOTES

APRIL

25 MONDAY

26 TUESDAY

27 WEDNESDAY

28 THURSDAY

APRIL/MAY

FRIDAY 29

SATURDAY 30

SUNDAY 1

NOTES

MAY

2 MONDAY

3 TUESDAY

4 WEDNESDAY

5 THURSDAY

MAY

FRIDAY 6

SATURDAY 7

SUNDAY 8

NOTES

MAY

9 MONDAY

10 TUESDAY

11 WEDNESDAY

12 THURSDAY

MAY

FRIDAY 13

SATURDAY 14

SUNDAY 15

NOTES

MAY

16 MONDAY

17 TUESDAY

18 WEDNESDAY

19 THURSDAY

MAY

FRIDAY 20

SATURDAY 21

SUNDAY 22

NOTES

MAY

23 MONDAY

24 TUESDAY

25 WEDNESDAY

26 THURSDAY

MAY

FRIDAY 27

SATURDAY 28

SUNDAY 29

NOTES

MAY/JUNE

30 MONDAY

31 TUESDAY

1 WEDNESDAY

2 THURSDAY

JUNE

FRIDAY 3

SATURDAY 4

SUNDAY 5

NOTES

JUNE

6 MONDAY

7 TUESDAY

8 WEDNESDAY

9 THURSDAY

JUNE

FRIDAY 10

SATURDAY 11

SUNDAY 12

NOTES

JUNE

13 MONDAY

14 TUESDAY

15 WEDNESDAY

16 THURSDAY

JUNE

FRIDAY 17

SATURDAY 18

SUNDAY 19

NOTES

JUNE

20 MONDAY

21 TUESDAY

22 WEDNESDAY

23 THURSDAY

JUNE

FRIDAY 24

SATURDAY 25

SUNDAY 26

NOTES

JUNE

27 MONDAY

28 TUESDAY

29 WEDNESDAY

30 THURSDAY

JULY
FRIDAY 1

SATURDAY 2

SUNDAY 3

NOTES

JULY

4 MONDAY

5 TUESDAY

6 WEDNESDAY

7 THURSDAY

JULY

FRIDAY 8

SATURDAY 9

SUNDAY 10

NOTES

JULY

11 MONDAY

12 TUESDAY

13 WEDNESDAY

14 THURSDAY

JULY
FRIDAY 15

SATURDAY 16

SUNDAY 17

NOTES

JULY

18 MONDAY

19 TUESDAY

20 WEDNESDAY

21 THURSDAY

JULY

FRIDAY 22

SATURDAY 23

SUNDAY 24

NOTES

JULY

25 MONDAY

26 TUESDAY

27 WEDNESDAY

28 THURSDAY

JULY

FRIDAY 29

SATURDAY 30

SUNDAY 31

NOTES

AUGUST

1 MONDAY

2 TUESDAY

3 WEDNESDAY

4 THURSDAY

AUGUST

FRIDAY 5

SATURDAY 6

SUNDAY 7

NOTES

AUGUST

8 MONDAY

9 TUESDAY

10 WEDNESDAY

11 THURSDAY

AUGUST

FRIDAY 12

SATURDAY 13

SUNDAY 14

NOTES

AUGUST

15 MONDAY

16 TUESDAY

17 WEDNESDAY

18 THURSDAY

AUGUST

FRIDAY 19

SATURDAY 20

SUNDAY 21

NOTES

AUGUST

22 MONDAY

23 TUESDAY

24 WEDNESDAY

25 THURSDAY

AUGUST

FRIDAY 26

SATURDAY 27

SUNDAY 28

NOTES

AUGUST/SEPTEMBER

29 MONDAY

30 TUESDAY

31 WEDNESDAY

1 THURSDAY

SEPTEMBER

FRIDAY 2

SATURDAY 3

SUNDAY 4

NOTES

SEPTEMBER

5 MONDAY

6 TUESDAY

7 WEDNESDAY

8 THURSDAY

SEPTEMBER

FRIDAY 9

SATURDAY 10

SUNDAY 11

NOTES

SEPTEMBER

12 MONDAY

13 TUESDAY

14 WEDNESDAY

15 THURSDAY

SEPTEMBER

FRIDAY 16

SATURDAY 17

SUNDAY 18

NOTES

SEPTEMBER

19 MONDAY

20 TUESDAY

21 WEDNESDAY

22 THURSDAY

SEPTEMBER

FRIDAY 23

SATURDAY 24

SUNDAY 25

NOTES

SEPTEMBER

26 MONDAY

27 TUESDAY

28 WEDNESDAY

29 THURSDAY

SEPTEMBER/OCTOBER

FRIDAY 30

SATURDAY 1

SUNDAY 2

NOTES

OCTOBER

3 MONDAY

4 TUESDAY

5 WEDNESDAY

6 THURSDAY

OCTOBER

FRIDAY 7

SATURDAY 8

SUNDAY 9

NOTES

OCTOBER

10 MONDAY

11 TUESDAY

12 WEDNESDAY

13 THURSDAY

OCTOBER

FRIDAY 14

SATURDAY 15

SUNDAY 16

NOTES

OCTOBER
17 MONDAY

18 TUESDAY

19 WEDNESDAY

20 THURSDAY

OCTOBER

FRIDAY 21

SATURDAY 22

SUNDAY 23

NOTES

OCTOBER

24 MONDAY

25 TUESDAY

26 WEDNESDAY

27 THURSDAY

OCTOBER

FRIDAY 28

SATURDAY 29

SUNDAY 30

NOTES

OCTOBER/NOVEMBER

31 MONDAY

1 TUESDAY

2 WEDNESDAY

3 THURSDAY

NOVEMBER

FRIDAY 4

SATURDAY 5

SUNDAY 6

NOTES

NOVEMBER

7 MONDAY

8 TUESDAY

9 WEDNESDAY

10 THURSDAY

NOVEMBER

FRIDAY 11

SATURDAY 12

SUNDAY 13

NOTES

NOVEMBER

14 MONDAY

15 TUESDAY

16 WEDNESDAY

17 THURSDAY

NOVEMBER

FRIDAY 18

SATURDAY 19

SUNDAY 20

NOTES

NOVEMBER

21 MONDAY

22 TUESDAY

23 WEDNESDAY

24 THURSDAY

NOVEMBER

FRIDAY 25

SATURDAY 26

SUNDAY 27

NOTES

NOVEMBER/DECEMBER

28 MONDAY

29 TUESDAY

30 WEDNESDAY

1 THURSDAY

DECEMBER

FRIDAY 2

SATURDAY 3

SUNDAY 4

NOTES

DECEMBER

5 MONDAY

6 TUESDAY

7 WEDNESDAY

8 THURSDAY

DECEMBER

FRIDAY 9

SATURDAY 10

SUNDAY 11

NOTES

DECEMBER

12 MONDAY

13 TUESDAY

14 WEDNESDAY

15 THURSDAY

DECEMBER

FRIDAY 16

SATURDAY 17

SUNDAY 18

NOTES

DECEMBER

19 MONDAY

20 TUESDAY

21 WEDNESDAY

22 THURSDAY

DECEMBER

FRIDAY 23

SATURDAY 24

SUNDAY 25

NOTES

DECEMBER

26 MONDAY

27 TUESDAY

28 WEDNESDAY

29 THURSDAY

DECEMBER

FRIDAY 30

SATURDAY 31

SUNDAY 1

NOTES

CONTACTS

NAME
PHONE
EMAIL
ADDRESS

NAME
PHONE
EMAIL
ADDRESS

NAME
PHONE
EMAIL
ADDRESS

NAME
PHONE
EMAIL
ADDRESS

CONTACTS

NAME
PHONE
EMAIL
ADDRESS

NAME
PHONE
EMAIL
ADDRESS

NAME
PHONE
EMAIL
ADDRESS

NAME
PHONE
EMAIL
ADDRESS

CONTACTS

NAME
PHONE
EMAIL
ADDRESS

NAME
PHONE
EMAIL
ADDRESS

NAME
PHONE
EMAIL
ADDRESS

NAME
PHONE
EMAIL
ADDRESS

CONTACTS

NAME
PHONE
EMAIL
ADDRESS

NAME
PHONE
EMAIL
ADDRESS

NAME
PHONE
EMAIL
ADDRESS

NAME
PHONE
EMAIL
ADDRESS

CONTACTS

NAME
PHONE
EMAIL
ADDRESS

NAME
PHONE
EMAIL
ADDRESS

NAME
PHONE
EMAIL
ADDRESS

NAME
PHONE
EMAIL
ADDRESS

CONTACTS

NAME
PHONE
EMAIL
ADDRESS

NAME
PHONE
EMAIL
ADDRESS

NAME
PHONE
EMAIL
ADDRESS

NAME
PHONE
EMAIL
ADDRESS

CONTACTS

NAME
PHONE
EMAIL
ADDRESS

NAME
PHONE
EMAIL
ADDRESS

NAME
PHONE
EMAIL
ADDRESS

NAME
PHONE
EMAIL
ADDRESS

CONTACTS

NAME
PHONE
EMAIL
ADDRESS

NAME
PHONE
EMAIL
ADDRESS

NAME
PHONE
EMAIL
ADDRESS

NAME
PHONE
EMAIL
ADDRESS

CONTACTS

NAME
PHONE
EMAIL
ADDRESS

NAME
PHONE
EMAIL
ADDRESS

NAME
PHONE
EMAIL
ADDRESS

NAME
PHONE
EMAIL
ADDRESS

CONTACTS

NAME
PHONE
EMAIL
ADDRESS

NAME
PHONE
EMAIL
ADDRESS

NAME
PHONE
EMAIL
ADDRESS

NAME
PHONE
EMAIL
ADDRESS

NOTES

NOTES

Notes

NOTES

NOTES

NOTES

NOTES

NOTES

NOTES

NOTES

NOTES

www.ingramcontent.com/pod-product-compliance
Lightning Source LLC
Chambersburg PA
CBHW060833220526
45466CB00003B/1083